Dear Sophie,

may all your
days be happy ones.

Love,
Grace

Happy Birthday!

The Art of Happiness

The Art of

Happiness

Selected Writings of

André Maurois

Edited by Karen Middaugh

♛ Hallmark Editions

Copyright © 1971 by Hallmark Cards, Inc.,
Kansas City, Missouri. All Rights Reserved.
Printed in the United States of America.
Library of Congress Catalog Card Number: 71-122364.
Standard Book Number: 87529-114-7.

The Art of Happiness

André Maurois: Realistic Optimist

André Maurois was an optimist — an optimist who preserved his serene outlook through war, tragedy, and the increasing tensions of the modern world. Through it all, he kept his belief that real happiness is possible for everyone.

But Maurois was at the same time a realist. He knew that love and happiness do not come automatically, but only after hard work and dedication. To become a great writer, he said, a man must be willing to spend long hours learning his art. That is the case with anything we do. If we wish to find satisfaction in our jobs, we must take pride in doing them as well as we can. To have a successful marriage, a couple must first determine to make it succeed, and then refuse to let trivial disagreements and problems stand in their way.

Throughout his works, Maurois constantly reaffirmed the value of man's traditional goals. Even in today's world, he believed, man must search for his happiness in the ordinary things of life — in his marriage, in his family, and with his friends. But even more, a man must search his heart and try to be honest with himself. When a man is at peace with himself, he will be able to find happiness in the world around him.

Friendship, Love and Marriage

Love, either of children, wife, or friends,

breaks the prison of loneliness.

The Art of Friendship

I would rather be betrayed by a false friend than deceive a true one.

*F*riendship, like marriage, implies a vow, which is indicated by Abel Bonnard's definition: "Friendship is the positive and unalterable choice of a person whom we have singled out for qualities that we most admire." There must be no conditions: once friends, always friends.

*A*nother essential attribute of friendship is, I believe, mutual admiration. "But," you will say, "I have friends whom I do not admire. I love them just the same, and would tell them frankly that I do not admire them." There is a confusion here and the need to probe more deeply into reality. We all have friends to whom we speak harsh truths, and indeed there can be no true friendship without this kind of sincerity. But if we can endure criticism from a friend, which, coming from another, would anger us, isn't it because we know that he admires us fundamentally? I do not mean that he thinks we possess all the virtues or that he finds us particularly intelligent. It is more complex than that. I mean that he has carefully considered our faults and our good qualities and has chosen us; better still, he has preferred us to others.

It is very important to realize that sincerity is possible only because of this admiration. We accept any criticism from him who loves or admires us because it does not impair the self-confidence without which our life would be unbearable. Great friendships between writers have been made possible by this alone. Louis Bouilhet sincerely criticized Flaubert, but Flaubert did not mind it because he knew that Bouilhet thought him a master. Heaven protect us from the "sincere friend" whose sincerity consists only of depressing us, who carefully warns us of the evil that is being spoken of us and seems to be afflicted with a peculiar deafness regarding the good.

In all circumstances we must defend our friends, not by denying evidence, for they are not saints and may have made mistakes, even serious ones, but by courageously affirming our fundamental respect. I know a woman who, whenever one of her intimates is attacked in her presence, merely states: "She is my friend," and refuses to say more. That, I believe, is true wisdom.

The Power of Love

A great love can endow the simplest person with discernment, abnegation, and self-assurance.

*T*he moment we succeed in forgetting ourselves entirely, the moment we lose ourselves, due to some mystical impulse, in some other existence, we find ourselves; and the events which do not concern this other existence become unimportant.

*D*eath itself is powerless to destroy the greatest love. Once in Spain I came across an old peasant woman of extraordinary dignity. "Oh," she said to me, "I have no cause to complain. Of course there's been trouble in my life; when I was twenty I fell in love with a young man; he loved me and we were married....He died in a few weeks, but just the same I had my share of happiness. For fifty years now I've lived thinking about him." What a consolation through years of sadness and loneliness always to be able to evoke at least one flawless memory! By means of perfect love like this, which fills our thoughts...with luminous images, as does a work of art or a religious faith, we share in something beyond our understanding. From the quick impact of our instincts a divine spark has been struck.

The last word concerning the art of loving comes from Mozart. Go to a concert; listen to those pure notes and those enchanting harmonies, and if your love then seems confused, harsh, and discordant, you are still unversed in the art of loving. But if, in your emotion, you are aware of this gradual acquisition of beauty, this marvelous understanding, this sublime reconciliation of conflicting and hostile themes beyond all dissonance, then you are embarked upon one of the few adventures in life that are worth having: a great love.

He who has not spent hours, days, or years with someone he loves cannot know what happiness is, for he is unable to imagine a protracted miracle like this — one which makes out of ordinary sights and events the most enchanted existence.

What is this soberer and gentler happiness which comes in the early moments of love to take its place by the side of desire, at first shyly but soon with a calm authority? Of what is this love made which is born of desire and outlives it? Of confidence, habit, and admiration. Almost all of our fellow beings deceive us, but a few of us have known the joy of meeting a woman or a man whose sincerity and frankness were genuine, who in almost every situation has behaved according to our wishes, and who in our most difficult moments has not forsaken us. Those few are familiar with that marvelous feeling: confidence. With at least one person they are able for a little while each day to lift the heavy visor of their helmets, breathe freely, and show their faces and their hearts without fear.

Two Different Sorts of Love

One day, when conversation turned on what really matters in life, Victor Hugo remarked that what he really valued was neither fame, fortune nor genius, but loving and being loved. He was right. Nothing is worth having unless it can be shared with those who love us and love us wholeheartedly, and yet their love adds nothing in itself unless we love them ourselves. Not that they need be many in number. I have often thought that one could be happy in the smallest town, even in some oasis in the Sahara, if only one had two or three real friends there; and contrawise I do not think that a head of state or a leading figure in the arts can know real happiness unless there is one person beside him with whom he can remove his mask. Hence the

12

enormously important part that intimate friends, wives or mistresses have played in the lives of great men. "One feels so alone," a famous man, around whom a little court revolved, once told me. Love, either of children, wife or friends, breaks the prison of loneliness.

But there are two different sorts of love. The first is selfish; that is to say, we form our attachments with an eye to what they may bring us. Some wives love, and truly love, a husband who gives them at once security, affection and sexual satisfaction, but they love him because they cannot conceive of a life without him. Such a husband is indispensable: he takes care of them and their children's happiness: he is the center of their life. But they hardly consider his life; they never ask themselves whether he has other desires or needs and they think it perfectly natural that his short span should be entirely spent in providing for the happiness of others.

There is no lack of husbands and lovers of the same sort. They too love a woman for what she gives them and never try to fathom her state of mind. Children who love their parents almost always love them in this way. To them their father is the person upon whom they can always rely, their mother the one to whom they can always confide, knowing she will always be on their side. But how many children make any attempt to lighten their parents' anxieties or to help them in difficulty? That is what I call selfish love.

To love a person for his or her own sake is to think not of what he or she gives us but what we give them. It is to implicate oneself so closely in their life and to share their feelings so completely that their happiness comes before our own. Do not, however, think this is something rare. Many parents are happier when their children succeed than they would have been at their own success. I have known plenty of married couples who lived for each other. Some friendships have been sublimely selfless. Balzac has portrayed one such in *Cousin Pons* and another in *Le Messe de l'Athée.* True friendship foresees the needs of others rather than proclaims its own. That is what I call loving people for their own sake.

The important point is that unselfish love brings more happiness than selfish love. Why? Because man is so made that forgetting himself helps to make him happy. As long as you think only of yourself you live in a state of worry and discontent. You are preoccupied with your own position: "Have I got all I could out of life? What mistake did I make to land me where I am? What do people think about me? Am I well liked?" But as soon as another person becomes the center of our life, our doubts are resolved. What must we do? We must try to make

14

those whom we love happier. From that moment life takes on a new meaning and revolves on this central axis. The extraordinary happiness given by a love for God is not, unfortunately, within the reach of all, but love for his creatures brings its own joy and reward.

The Sweet Monotony of Marriage

"What would you call a marriage in which the husband is entitled to only one wife?"

The young girl to whom this question was put by her teacher answered, "Monotony."

The student was not far wrong, but I would like to show that monotony is the most charming part of married life; that it is more apparent than real....

A long time ago, Honoré de Balzac, a true bachelor, always ready for courtship with some lady, was deeply attracted by the idea of getting married, yet was afraid to do so. A very wise friend of his, a married woman faithful to her husband, slipped this remark into one of her letters: "You must not think that life always needs new aspects. You must understand what treasures you can find in the fact that this hour — such a pleasant one — will be the same tomorrow, then later, and always. Dried-up souls will find there only boredom; for ordinary people it will represent...a pleasure; but for you, you may find in such an hour the greatest refinement."

What a pretty sentence! It is true that life does not offer anything prettier than its hues, and it is on the landscape of a quiet life that these hues take on their loveliest colors.

To give a present to your wife or husband on an anniversary is a mere ritual. But to choose a gift with love, to guess the wishes of your partner, to run from shop to shop to find the exact present that will bring fulfillment creates a real rainbow of pleasure whose hues delight both partners. There is quite a difference, and such a nice one at that, if, when you have a new frock, your husband's eyes are sharp enough to notice it and pay you a compliment before you have had time to ask him if he likes it. The wife who is capable of listening with interest to the description, repeated and repeated, of the future hopes of her husband, brings a sweet hue to their relationship and soothes the careworn mind.

In marriage there cannot be complete monotony, since a couple travels together through space and time, with new events and new people always to be found. Each year, each season, brings fresh hues to married love. Couples, like nature, have their burgeoning spring, their glorious summer, their melancholy fall. Together, husband and wife discover new landscapes and new countries on holiday trips which give new shades to love. A couple is not the same in Spain as in Sweden; at the seaside as in the mountains.

On the long road of life, new friends bring new ideas, new riches, sometimes also new dangers, but dangers that animate the daily routine. Whoever loves with strength learns, when necessary, how to renew himself. Each day you empty your bag of seductions. Nevertheless, seducing remains necessary, and you manage to find other means of seduction. Even old age is full of delightful hues. A pretty face ages well, and one takes pleasure in finding, beneath the crown of white hair, the smile you loved when the curls were fair or dark. Marriage is by no means a monotonous affair, for the partners themselves change. When you marry you don't become linked to a single woman or a single man; you are bound to all the women or all the men she or he will become.

Let's also say that monotony has some aspects that are rapturous and touching. Zulma Carraud was right indeed when she underlined to Honoré de Balzac the fact that it is soothing to think how similar the hour a couple lives is to other hours to come. Yes, similar to the hours of tomorrow, and the day after tomorrow, and to any future day....

After many years of marriage, the intimacy between a couple is so close that each guesses what the other is thinking and will say. In fact, a happy husband journeys in his wife's thoughts in the same way that he traverses his garden slowly each evening after dinner....He awaits the same sentence at the same place, knowing that at such and such a bend of the lane he will see blossoming red roses. The roses are always of the same red and the words of the sentence full of the same harmony. Oh marvelous sweetness of monotony!

Building a Happy Marriage

True holiness lies more in humility, sweetness, and charity, than in religious ecstasies and mortifications. Similarly, true love may be recognized, not by the violent assaults of passionate desire, but by the perfect and lasting harmony of daily life.

It is a formidable decision to make when one says: "I bind myself for life; I have chosen; from now on my aim will be not to search for someone who may please me, but to please the one I have chosen." Yet this decision can alone produce a successful marriage, and if the vow is not sincere the couple's chances for happiness are very slim, for it will run the risk of disruption when the first obstacles and the inevitable difficulties of life in common are encountered.

Whether it be the marriage of two people or the government of a nation, it must be realized that perfection can never be achieved and that, if it could be by some miracle of love, it would not last. We can only try patiently and continually to approximate perfection. It is quite useless to marry as one buys a lottery ticket, saying to oneself: "Who knows? Perhaps I'll be happy." Much better to do it as an artist undertakes the creation of a work of art. "This is a novel," the husband and wife should both say, "which I am going to live, not write. I know that I must take into account the peculiarities of the two characters who are already drawn, but I want to succeed and I will succeed...."

Marriage is not something that can be accomplished all at once; it has to be constantly reaccomplished. A couple must never indulge in idle tranquillity with the remark: "The game is won; let's relax." The game is never won. The chances of life are such that anything is possible.... Marriage is an edifice that must be rebuilt every day....

Nothing in our daily life will last if neglected; houses, stuffs, friendships, pleasures. Roofs fall in, love comes to an end. A tile needs refastening, a joint must be repaired, a misunderstanding cleared up. Otherwise bitterness is created; feelings deep down in the soul become centers of infection, and one day, during a quarrel, the abscess breaks and each is horrified by the picture of himself or herself discovered in the other's mind.

No marriage can be a happy one unless tastes are mutually respected. Once again, it is absurd to imagine that two people can have the same thoughts, the same opinions, and the same wishes. The thing is impossible, and it is also undesirable. During the honeymoon, as we have said, the two lovers want to believe that they are alike in all ways. Inevitably the moment arrives when strong characters resume their rights. "If one wants marriage to be a refuge," says Alain, "friendship must gradually replace love." Replace it? No — the matter is more complex. In a truly happy marriage there must be a mingling of friendship and love, and here the closeness of friendship takes on an indescribable quality of indulgence and affection. Two people recognize that they are morally and intellectually unlike, but they joyfully accept the differences in their temperaments, discovering therein an opportunity for spiritual development....

Rochefoucauld's phrase is classic: "There are good marriages, but no exquisite ones." I hope I have shown that there can be exquisite ones; but these are not by any means the easiest. How could the life of two people together ever be easy when both are subject to fits of bad temper, mistakes, and illnesses which spoil their dispositions? A marriage without conflicts is almost as inconceivable as a nation without crises. But when love has pleaded its first cases and affection has changed indignation into tender and amused indulgence, perhaps the crises will be fairly easily dealt with.

Thus marriage is not at all what romantic lovers imagine it to be; it is an institution founded upon an instinct; to be successful, it requires not only physical attraction but willpower, patience, and the always difficult acceptance of "the other"; if these conditions are fulfilled, a beautiful and lasting affection can be established — a unique and, to those who have never known it, incomprehensible mingling of love, friendship, sensuality, and respect, without which there is no true marriage.

*I*s there an art of not tiring people? The great secret is to allow them to be natural. An unnatural attitude is difficult to maintain without a loss of attraction. Wise lovers strive to preserve their companions' natural propensities. There are men who hope to mould women, impose tastes and ideas.

This is sheer folly. If we find a woman too different from our ideal, let us not love her; but if we have definitely chosen her, we must not hinder her development. In friendship and also in love, we are happy to see those with whom it is possible to be ourselves without embarrassment or pretense.

There are several rules which should be followed by both sexes in learning the art of not tiring the loved one. The first is to show in the most intimate moments as much politeness as during the first encounter. Well-born people are courteous by nature. All things may be said graciously and to imagine brutality to be the only satisfactory expression of frankness is a strange confusion. The second is to maintain a sense of humor under all conditions, to be able to make fun of oneself, to realize the puerility of most disagreements, and not to attach a tragic importance to accumulated grievances. It is useless to aggravate a present torment with memories of past quarrels.

$\mathcal{D}$omestic life has a way of producing awkward daily problems. I believe that these problems can be solved through humor, affection and above all the firm resolve to hold the relationship together. It is not a matter of saying, "Can we live together?" but of insisting, "We must and we want to live together," and then of finding the ways and means. This brings us to our subject: good manners in marriage.

Above all, husband and wife should aim to be specially indulgent in the presence of others. Each has a stock of ideas, anecdotes and memories which are familiar to the other.... A husband (or a wife) must not always expect his spouse to say something new, but rather that each in his way should sparkle in the public eye. They must be able to listen to each other without real or apparent boredom and even with pleasure....

One should exert at least as much tact with one's husband (or one's wife) as with friends, and even more with people one doesn't know. It is essential that married couples should share confidence and mutual respect for each other. Frankness is all very well. Yes, we pretend we like it.... But only the frankness of those who, when they are being frank, say that they love us just as we are.

Communion in Marriage

Religious faith, national or political faith, or faith in the necessity and beauty of a lifework, if shared, is a marvelous strengthening of love. It is indeed difficult for a passionate believer to experience a permanent emotion for the person who does not in any way share his beliefs, and in such a case infinite tact and respect are required of the unbeliever, or the hope of conversion must be present in the mind of the other — a conversion which frequently follows love — if such love is to persist. One may be assured of happiness by sharing without reserve the faith of the man or woman one loves. In this way our intellectual as well as our emotional force propels us in the chosen direction. All work done with love as a motive is delightful, but nothing in the world can equal the joy of a true mingling of work and love. Of this perfect mingling are sometimes produced those amazing pairs of scholars, artists, apostles, who are not couples but teams. Here courtship is useless; communion has taken its place.

A married woman's best friend should be her husband, and a married man's best friend his wife.

Some couples are so closely related that even the frankest and most intimate confidences seem quite natural. If *he* has a complaint to make, he tells *her* and not a third person because he knows that it will be received with humor, sympathy and intelligence. Perfect friendship between man and woman must satisfy heart and mind, as well as body. Now it is marriage that makes this possible. When a husband is his wife's best friend she can safely have other men friends, too, if she wishes....

There is, in fact, a fundamental difference between love and friendship. Love is blind, jealous, exacting and often unjust. Friendship, on the other hand, is equitable, generous and intelligent. Love is changeable, surging and drifting on the waves of passion, but friendship takes a smooth and peaceful course.... Marriage alone can transform love into friendship without killing love in the process. On the contrary, love can — and should — become something that one has built up, brick by brick, throughout a lifetime. Don't confuse desire and passion.... Desire is nature's gift to two young people, whereas passion is the brief folly which makes us look at someone through distorted eyes. Marriage provides instead a tenderness and understanding, a *compassion* that recognizes the partner as he really is, with all his faults and virtues, and yet loves him nonetheless.

"Remember to forget," said a philosopher, and that is wise advice. Each day brings its own problem. One must live in the present instead of constantly dragging up the past, which nothing can now change. We must also say to our pessimist: "Remember not to expect the worst." One must prepare sensibly for the future, if one can, but without foreboding of misery and worry which has not yet happened. Don't mourn for tomorrow or what it may bring, because in the emotional sphere it does not exist.... There is no tomorrow, only the present. Husbands and wives, try to live in the present. And if the present is happy, then your marriage will be happy today. Don't expect any more. This life is lived from day to day.

The
Art of
Family Life

*F*amily life offers

an apprenticeship to love....

The Importance of Family Life

The art of family life is extremely important. Badly brought up children can sometimes remould their own characters; occasionally their lack of equilibrium results in genius; but we can assure them an easier life if we know how to give them a serene and happy childhood. A happy childhood is one which is presided over by united parents who love their children tenderly, impose a steady discipline, and see to it that a conspicuous equality between them is preserved. Inevitable changes in character occur at stated periods; advice must be widely and sparingly given, and the most effective advice is the setting of a good example. Finally, it is necessary to freshen the family atmosphere by letting in draughts of air from the outside world.

A question must now be asked: is family life an institution that will endure? I believe it to be irreplaceable for the same reasons that marriage is irreplaceable, because it moulds individual instinct into social sensibility. It is a sound idea to spend early years away from the family, but to almost every man, after years of apprenticeship to life and inevitable adventuring, the moment comes when he returns with joy to those natural affections. After difficult days spent in an indifferent or cruel world, students, philosophers, cabinet ministers, soldiers, and artists are happy to become again children, parents, grandparents, or simply men, when they sit down to their evening meal in the family circle.

Happiness in Family Life

Family life offers an apprenticeship to love and it is because of this that, despite our grievances, we experience a strange happiness in returning to it. But this remembered apprenticeship is not the only cause of the trustful feeling with which we return. The family hearth is also the place where, as Valéry says, we can be ourselves.

Is this such a great and unusual advantage? Can we not be ourselves wherever we please? Certainly not. In life we must play a role; we have chosen an attitude; we have been assigned a character. We have official capacities to fill; social life makes demands upon us. For a large part of their lives, bishops, professors, and businessmen (among many others) have no right to be themselves.

Without a family, man, alone in the world, trembles with the cold. In countries where family life, for various reasons, is less intensified, men feel the need to draw closer to their fellows and think with the crowd in order to compensate for the loss of that warm and friendly little group.

Education of Children

The most frequent of the seemingly harmless mistakes for which parents are responsible is to spoil a child, that is, to allow it to believe itself all-powerful when it merely seems to be so because of its parents' weaknesses. Nothing is more dangerous. The formation of a child's character begins during the first months of its life. In a year it will have become either amenable to discipline or it will not respond to it at all. I have often heard people say..., "One has very little influence upon one's children. Their characters are what they are and one can do nothing to change them."

But in many cases it would have been possible to change them by means of that early education to which little thought is given. During the first days of its existence, an infant must be made to live by rule; suffering will be its eventual fate if it responds to no discipline. Society has its unchanging laws. Each must cut his own path with hatchet and bill-hook — a painful task, requiring patience, submission, and tenacity. The spoiled child lives in a world of fantasy; he believes until the end of his life that a smile or an angry gesture will produce the desired results. He wants to be loved unselfishly as he was loved by parents who were not firm enough with him. We have all known adult spoiled children: men who reach high positions and then lose them through childish behavior; women of sixty who still believe that they can obtain what they want by sulking. The remedy here is for the mother to teach the infant, during those first months when it is getting its...wordless instruction in living, that there are rules to be complied with.

*E*ven in those of us who have at last admitted the heedlessness of nature and the defensive selfishness of other men, there often survives a childish sadness and a melancholy regret for the illusions of early years. We know that the world in which we live is imperfect, but we imagine it as another, wherein we shall be able to find once more the golden age of our childhood. True maturity, true wisdom, are attained only by those who can wholeheartedly say with Marcus Aurelius, "All that accords with thee, O world, accords with myself," or with Descartes, "I have made it my habit to vanquish my desires rather than the order of the world, and to think that what has not happened is, with regard to myself, something totally impossible."

31

*I*t is important that children should feel themselves equally loved and by both parents; also that they should never be allowed to discover the existence of hostility between their parents. Such things cause them suffering, then loss of respect. People who rebel against everything in later life are often those who, as children, observed a wide difference between the preaching and the practice of their parents. A daughter who is contemptuous of her mother will feel similarly towards all women. A tyrannical father may be responsible for his children's (especially his daughters') conception of marriage as a kind of slavery. It seems to me that a father should desire above all things to give his children the greatest amount of happiness compatible with the kind of life they are destined to lead. This maximum of happiness is necessary because life is short and childhood memories are their most precious possessions, and also because the misery of a repressed and gloomy childhood may be carried over into later life.

At the same time, a father must be firm; he must make his children realize from their earliest days that the world cannot be conquered easily, for, if they do not, great disappointments are in store for them. I have known boys so well protected from the world by their mothers that their first encounters with rough, heartless comrades plunge them into despair. They are incapable of coping with life and are apt to abandon themselves to failure. To insist upon the strict observance of a few rules regarding work and behavior, and at the same time to do everything possible to insure a child's happiness seems to me the best way to make certain that the transition from childhood to adolescence will be accomplished with a minimum of suffering.

The Problems of Growing Up

The most secret tragedies, and perhaps the most poignant, are played out in those school playgrounds where, every day, some ten-year-old Hamlet discovers injustice, envy, malice, outruns them, accepts them, and becomes a man.

When parents see what difficulties their children meet with during their first contacts with real life, they remember their own mistakes; they are anxious to protect their loved ones and they naively attempt to give them the benefit of their own experiences. But these experiences are rarely of any use to others. Everyone must live out his own life;

ideas change with the passing years. The sort of wisdom that comes with old age cannot be acquired by a young man.

Experience is valuable only when it has brought suffering and when the suffering has left its mark upon both body and mind. Sleepless nights and conflicts with reality make statesmen realists; how could these experiences be usefully handed on to young idealists who expect to transform the universe without effort? The counsels of Polonius are platitudes, but the moment we start giving advice we are all like Polonius. For us, those platitudes are packed with meaning, memories, and visions. For our children, they are abstract and boring. We should like to make a wise woman of a girl of twenty; it is physiologically impossible. "The counsels of old age," said Vauvenargues, "are like a winter's sun which gives light but no warmth."

*D*uring our children's adolescence we must try to recall our own and not complain of them for having the thoughts, feeling, and moods that belong to adolescence. This is difficult. At twenty we all say: "If I ever have children, I'll be able to get close to them and be the sort of father that my own was incapable of being." But at fifty we resemble our own parents fairly closely and in their turn our children, as we so greatly desired (and so uselessly), will resemble us; but this will be when we are no longer there and when their role on earth will be similar to our own.

One sees how all these conflicts and grievances produce the awkward age. A very young child goes through what may be called the fairyland age when food, warmth, and play are benefits received from ministering deities. To many children, the discovery of the outside world and the necessity for work come as a shock. Friends are made at school and the child begins to see his family through their eyes. He realizes that the people he has always taken for granted and who were as necessary to him as air and water may seem wonderful or insignificant to other children. Many new relationships are formed; the bonds uniting him to his parents relax, but they never break. At this period, people outside the family have their greatest influence and this is as it should be. At this period also the child turns

35

rebel, but his parents must keep on loving him.

I have pointed out that family life will be very matter-of-fact and dull without the influence of religion and the arts. The adolescent, always an idealist, is offended by the Polonius-like advice of his father. He curses the family and its laws. He wants juster ones. He thinks of love as a great and beautiful thing, and he needs friendship and affection. It is a time of vows and secret confidences; it is also a time of disappointments, for vows are not kept, confidences are betrayed, and lovers are inconstant. He wants to do well and things always turn out badly. His cynicism comes from frustrated idealism and the disparity between his dreams and the reality about him.

It is a tragic and difficult period in every life. Young men have many ideas but no responsibilities. They do not find themselves in daily conflict with men and things; they have no family to support, no business to run, no public responsibilities. They work with words and phrases only, and this gives them an abstract idea of the world, frequently exalted but always inexact. Women and society are very different from their imaginings and this makes them unhappy. But they soon come out of adolescence; then marriage and the birth of their children strengthen and support their dangerous abstract intelligence with family responsibilities. Little by little, after a difficult apprenticeship in family, business, and public life, they will become real men and will be able to help their adolescent children through similar experiences.

The Family and the Outside World

It is a bad thing for a family to keep too much to itself; fresh currents should flow into it as into a bay wide open to the sea. The outsider may be invisible, his actual presence is not necessary. He may be a great musician or a great poet. Daily reading of the Bible moulds the minds of numerous Protestant families. Many of the best English writers owed their style to this continual reading of a great book, and if there are a number of women in England today who have a natural gift for writing, it is perhaps because they have been sheltered by this religious reading from too much family small talk and made familiar at an early age with a noble style. Madame de Sévigné and Madame de La Fayette and other French ladies of the seventeenth century were similarly trained by their studies of Latin. Some families fall into the dangerous habit of never finishing their sentences; they understand one another easily with few words and make no effort whatever. To combat this evil the intellectual level should be raised by continual familiarity with the best things humanity has produced. With sincere religious convictions, a love of the arts (especially music), a common political faith, and some sort of shared work, a family may be lifted above itself.

Another danger is that a family always has difficulty in taking one of its members seriously. This is neither hostility nor jealousy; it is merely that the family is accustomed to regarding him in a different light. Read the lives of the Brontë sisters. They were not novelists in their father's estimation. What was to them their work and their art seemed to Mr. Brontë merely a game, and importance of which he was far from realizing. Tolstoy's wife recognized his genius; his children admired him and tried to understand him. But in spite of their efforts, wife and children saw in him the human being full of peculiarities and absurdities just as clearly as they did the great writer. To the Countess Tolstoy he was the man who said that it was not right to have servants and then asked her at the eleventh hour to provide luncheon for fifteen guests.

I have said that one could be oneself in the family circle. Yes, but it is not possible to be anyone else in that intimate atmosphere; one cannot rise above oneself. The excessively pious and the heroic have no place there. The members of a family may not underrate a genius in their midst, but they minimize him by their manner of appreciating, which is not understanding but delighting in the fact that there is such a man in the family. If a Jones becomes a great preacher or a great statesman, the Joneses rejoice, not because they are moved by the sermons or believe in...their kinsman's reforms, but because they are proud to have the Jones name appear in the newspapers. The aged aunt listens to the lectures of her geographer nephew, not because she likes geography but because she is fond of her nephew.

The leveling influence of mediocrity and the denial of the supreme importance of the mind's development account for many revolts against family life. There are many occasions when great men are convinced that, in order to fulfill their destinies, they must escape from the warmth and indulgence of their own families. At one of these moments, Tolstoy embraces a monastic life; a boy hears the call: "Thou shalt abandon thy father and thy mother"; Gauguin quits his family to live in Tahiti as the monk of painting. Each one of us, at least once in our life, has heard the inner call of the eldest brother and has felt himself to be the prodigal son.

I believe the advantages of such escape to be imaginary. To flee from one's family, that is, from ties which bind us to our own people, at first natural and then voluntary, is to establish other ties that are less natural, for man was not made to live alone; he may go into monastic or literary seclusion where there is also indulgence, servitude, and abandon; or he may drift, like Nietzsche, into madness. True wisdom, as Marcus Aurelius knew so well, cannot be acquired by withdrawing from the world. To escape from family life is easy but useless; to elevate family life is a more difficult and a nobler thing to do.

The Search for Happiness

Instead of lamenting

    the absurdity of the world,

        let us try to transform the corner

    of it into which we were born.

The Guidelines of Life

*L*et me begin by recalling to you a few rules, as old as civilization, which hold true in spite of technological inventions and nihilistic philosophies.

The first is that *a man must live for something besides himself.* The man who thinks about himself finds a thousand reasons for being unhappy. He has not done that which he ought and meant to have done; he has not been rewarded according to his merits; he is not loved in the way of which he had dreamed. Dwelling on the past can lead only to vain regrets and remorse. "Our faults are fated to be forgotten, and they deserve no more." Instead of harking back to a past that cannot be wiped out, try to build up a present in which you may take pride tomorrow. To be at odds with oneself is the worst of evils. A man who lives for something outside: for his country, for his work, for a woman, for the hungry and persecuted, is oblivious of petty cares and anxieties. "The real outside world is the real inside world."

The second rule is *action.* Instead of lamenting the absurdity of the world, let us try to transform the corner of it into which we were born. We can't change the universe, but then who wants to change it? Our objective is simpler and closer at hand: to choose our trade and master it. Everyone has his own sphere. I write books, a carpenter puts together my bookcases, a policeman directs traffic, an engineer builds bridges, a mayor administers a town. And if they know their jobs, the more they have to do the happier they are. Indeed, they fill their leisure time with such apparently unnecessary activities as sports. And a football player sprawling in the mud is actually happy. As for our more useful actions, their efficiency is a source of joy. An energetic mayor makes for a clean town, an active priest makes for a lively parish, and their success affords them satisfaction.

The third rule is *to believe in the power of free will.* The future is not entirely pre-determined; great men change the course of history and any one of us can to some extent modify that of his own life. No one, of course, is all-powerful; our freedom is limited, straddling as it does the dividing line between the humanly possible and the individual will. I can't prevent war, but my words and actions, multiplied by millions of others', may make war less likely to occur. At least I can refrain from telling my fellow countrymen, at the drop of a hat, that the national honor has been offended and that they must immolate themselves, along with the nation. It's not up to me to win battles; I have only to fight bravely on the ground where I stand. And since "will is limited only by daring," I must, heedless of its limitation, rule over myself the best I can. Laziness and cowardice are surrenders; hard work and courage are the results of determination. Indeed, will may be the first of the virtues.

Nevertheless, I propose as a fourth rule a virtue as precious as will, and that is steadfastness or fidelity, fidelity to your promises and engagements, fidelity to others and to yourself. *You must never be disappointing.* Fidelity is not easy; a thousand temptations waylay a word that has been given. "What?" you may say; "If I've married a foolish and unfaithful woman, do I have to be faithful to her? If I've chosen a profession that doesn't pan out, can't I take up another? If the political party of my choice turns out to be corrupt, can't I give it up and turn to one which I now know is more honest?" No. Loyalty shouldn't be blind. But we must beware of blaming our infidelities upon a mistaken judgment when they may be attributed, rather, to a lack of generosity. "The truth is," Alain tells us, "that any choice is mistaken if we abandon it, and that any choice is proved good by our goodwill. No one has sufficient reasons for the choice of his profession, because he can't know what it involves until after he has embraced it. Likewise no one chooses his loves." But it is possible to mould the woman of our choice, to do well at our...profession and to reform a...party. Fidelity creates its own justification.

44

I suppose that these rules of life seem to you both summary and severe. I understand, but there are no others. I don't ask you to live like a recluse or a Stoic. Cultivate a sense of humor; learn to smile at yourself — and at me. Accept your weaknesses, if you can't overcome them, but try to keep a strong framework and underpinnings. A society in which the citizens live only for their vices and ambitions, a society that tolerates violence and injustice, a society in which men have no confidence in one another and have lost their will, is doomed to perish. Ancient Rome flourished as long as it had heroes; when it ceased to respect the values that had made for its greatness the Roman Empire went under. Scientific discoveries change the ways of action, but they do not alter its value or the reason behind it. So it was in the beginning and so it shall be forever.

To love the fine people about me, to avoid the wicked, to rejoice in good, endure evil — and to remember to forget: this is my optimism. It has helped me to live.

What Is Happiness?

The life that matters is all around you, in the flowers of your garden, in the little lizard sunning himself on your balcony, in the children looking tenderly at their mother, in the embracing lovers, in the house where a family eats and loves and plays games together. Nothing is more important than these humble lives which, added together, make up humanity.

If men could regard the events of their own lives with more open minds, they would frequently discover that they did not really desire the things they failed to obtain. There is a great difference between spoken wishes such as: "I should like to get married ... to be a senator ... to paint a good portrait," and actual burning desires which consume one's whole being. The latter make themselves known by acts. Unless the desire is absolutely impossible and absurd, it may frequently be achieved if enough determination is used. A man who desires honors obtains honors; he who wants friends gets them; a woman who desires conquests makes conquests. The young Bonaparte wanted power; the obstacles to its achievement seemed insurmountable; he surmounted them.

Of course, there are many cases where circumstances render success impossible; it is not easy to move the universe, and the difficulty frequently lies in the man himself. He *thinks* he desires to achieve a definite result, but some inner force pulls him in the opposite direction. How often have writers said to me that they would like to write such and such books if the kind of life they led did not make it impossible. If they passionately desired to write the books, they would lead different lives. Evidence of Balzac's strength of will and devotion to his work can be found in the kind of life he led or, more precisely, in the work itself.

I am, I admit, an optimist; but I do not believe, like Voltaire's Pangloss, that all is for the best in this best of all possible worlds. I know the horrors and difficulties of life: I have had my share of them. But I refuse to regard humanity's condition as terrible. True, we are spinning on a lump of dirt in illimitable space, without being too sure why; true, we will surely die. To me this is a set of facts, a situation to be accepted courageously. The only problem is: What can we do, and what ought we to do, while we are here?

Sources of Unhappiness

No great amount of experience is required to discover that the greedy search for money or success will almost always lead men into unhappiness. Why? Because that kind of life makes them depend upon things outside themselves. No one is more vulnerable than the ambitious man; some incident he knows nothing of, or some remark incorrectly repeated, will turn an influential man against him or cause a nation to persecute him. He will say that he had bad luck, that fate was against him. Fate is always against those who seek benefits, the acquiring of which does not depend upon themselves. That was in the lot also. The gods are justified.

Greed and ambition place us in conflict with our fellowmen, but it is far worse to be in conflict with ourselves. For we are happy when we can examine yesterday's actions and those of our whole life and say, "Perhaps I have acted unwisely; I may have been mistaken, but I did my best and I followed my own ideas. What I have said I can say again, or if my ideas have changed I can admit without shame that there were good reasons for my errors which were due to listening to incorrect information, or to my own faulty reasoning." When this interior harmony exists, the need for painful self-communion vanishes.

In reality, this agreement with oneself is somewhat rare. There are, in each one of us, two beings: a member of society and a human being with passionate feelings — an intellect and an animal. It is very unpleasant to realize that we are a prey to self-indulgence and that we are wise men only during a part of our lives. A harmonious agreement with oneself is difficult to achieve because many of our thoughts have very different origins from the ones we like to give them. We pretend that we are talking reasonably when, with false judgment and weak arguments, we are merely working off an old grudge. We are hostile to a certain group of people because one of its members has done us some serious injury. We refuse to admit these weaknesses, but our conscience tells us that they exist and we become dissatisfied with ourselves, we become bitter, violent, absurd, and we insult our friend because we know we are not the men we should have liked to be. Whence the importance of Socrates' "Know thyself." In order to achieve serenity, the intelligent man must first make objective all thought-distorting passions and memories.

You've been told that we're living on the edge of a precipice and that once we are aware of this we are fatally dizzy. But men have always lived, loved, worked and created on the edge of a precipice, and there's no reason why you should not follow their example....

The catastrophes that hang over us are of man's own creation, and by an effort of man's will they can be averted. Even if we are on the edge of a precipice we are not obliged to leap.

Another cause of unhappiness is the fear of danger. I do not mean to say that certain fears are not legitimate and even necessary. A man who is not careful to avoid being hit by a swiftly moving automobile will die on account of this lack of visual imagination. A nation which does not fear armed and hostile neighbors will soon be enslaved. But fears serve no purpose when they concern unpredictable events. We all know men who are so apprehensive of illness that their lives are destroyed. The man who is afraid that his money will be lost imagines the various ways in which he can be ruined and deprives himself of present happiness in order to be ready for misfortunes which, if they occurred, would merely reduce him to the state in which his fear has placed him. The jealous man foresees dangerous encounters with other men for the woman he loves; he struggles to put these imaginings from him and in the end he kills her love with his crazy watchfulness and thus brings on the catastrophe he feared.

The acute mental suffering caused by fear is all the more useless because anticipation is usually far worse than actuality. Illness is horrible, but it is less so than we are led to expect from the spectacle of our afflicted fellow beings, because fever and the habit of illness create, as it were, another body which reacts differently. Many of us are afraid of death, but nothing that we imagine regarding our death can be true; for all we know, we may die suddenly; also in normal cases the natural phenomenon of death has its various corresponding physical states. I remember distinctly meeting with an accident which might have been fatal. I lost consciousness, but the memory I have of the few seconds... preceding the accident is not a painful one.

Happiness Through Work

Whatever the object of your attention the same rules hold true. You must, *"learn to do the smallest thing in the grandest manner...."*

Do you see what I am driving at? Your aim should not be to "succeed," in the sense of making a good show. Success may well be a by-product of your effort, but again it may not be. The thing is to perform your chosen job as well as you are able.

The important thing to remember in regard to manual work is this: whether the work be simple or complicated, it can be well or badly done. There are clever and stupid ways of digging a trench, just as there are careful and neglectful ways of preparing a lecture. A stenographer may do mediocre or excellent work; it depends upon her technique, her care of her typewriter, her spacing of headings and the size of her page, and the attention she gives to rereading. If she tries to make her work a little better than is required of her, she becomes an artist at once and finds herself rewarded for her gratuitous efforts by deep and lasting satisfaction. She has not done this additional work for an employer, but for her self-respect and her own enjoyment; it is therefore done freely.

The pleasure of working may become so complete that it often succeeds in replacing all others. In my efforts to imagine Paradise, there enters my mind no vision of a place where winged souls do little else than sing and play their harps, but rather one of a study where I work everlastingly at some marvelous novel of infinite length with the keen power and precision that I could so rarely command upon earth. The Paradise of the gardener is a garden; a carpenter's is a bench.

An excellent example of the mingling of manual work and brain work is that of the housewife when she puts her heart into the accomplishment of her duties. A woman who runs her house well is both a queen and its subject. She is the one who makes work possible for her husband and children; she protects them from worries, feeds them and cares for them. She is Minister of Finance, and, thanks to her, the household budget is balanced. She is Minister of Fine Arts, and it is her doing if the house or apartment has charm. She is Minister of Family Education and responsible for the boys' entry into school and college and the girls' cleverness and cultivation.

A woman should be as proud of her success in making her house into a perfect little world as the greatest statesman of his in organizing a nation's affairs.... A perfect thing is perfect, whatever its dimensions. There is no repose for women except in families who have too much money. A two-day holiday from shop or workroom means two days spent in cleaning, washing, mending, and caring for the children. There are always urgent things to be done, to which must always be added her efforts not to look too plain, to dress nicely, and to improve her mind. A woman's job, if well done, leaves few moments of leisure, but its rewards are immediate. It is extraordinary to see how, in a few days, with very little money and plenty of courage, a clever woman can transform a hovel into a delightful place to live in. This is where the arts of working and loving intersect.

The Secret of Happiness

We live, eat, love, procreate, work. Why? Goethe answered: "In order to raise as high as possible the pyramid of my existence, whose base was given to me ready-made." A noble aim this, to try to make your life into a masterpiece.

Men are easily deceived. For a few vague words they imagine themselves to be under attack, they hate and kill one another. As far as you can, call them back to the life that matters, to its simple pleasures and affections.

And choose, on your own part, to live, rather than to act out a role in which you don't believe in a tragicomedy. Life is too short to be petty.

One of the most serious obstacles to happiness is the awkwardness of modern man, with his mind full of doctrines and abstract formulas, when he attempts to re-establish contact with real emotions. Animals and unsophisticated people achieve happiness more naturally, because their desires are simpler.... Civilized man, a parrot enslaved by his chattering, ceaselessly inoculates himself with loves and hatreds which he does not actually feel.

In this disorder from which spring so many imaginary misfortunes, the artist can help us to recapture real emotions better than the philosopher. Mystical knowledge alone, whether it be of art, love, or religion, gets at the essence of things; it alone brings stability, peace, and happiness. The artist who tries to capture the beauty of a landscape and whose gaze seems to dart out toward it in order that he may not miss a single detail knows perfect happiness while he is working. In his *Christmas Carol,* Dickens shows how a wretched, egotistical old man finds happiness, until then beyond his comprehension, because he allows himself to become fond of several people and through them is able to cast off his worst fault. Whenever we catch a fleeting glimpse of the extraordinary unity of the universe; when the motionless hills, the rustling trees, the swallows darting across the sky, and the insect crawling upon the windowpane suddenly become a part of our life and our life a part of the world about us, then we are aware, in a flash of intuition, of that love of the universe so greatly surpassing submission to it, which is expressed in the *Hymn to Joy.*

"Do you wish to know the secret of happiness?" Several years ago in the agony column of the London *Times* this question was asked, and all those who replied received an envelope containing two verses from Saint Matthew: "Ask, and it shall be given you; seek, and ye shall find; knock, and it shall be opened unto you: For every one that asketh receiveth; and he that seeketh findeth; and to him that knocketh it shall be opened." Such, actually, is the secret of happiness, and the ancients had the same idea in another form when they declared that Hope was left at the bottom of Pandora's box when all the evils had taken flight. He who seeks love shall find it; he who devotes himself unreservedly to friendship shall have friends; only the man who desires happiness with his whole heart shall find it.

Early in life we put questions in an unanswerable form: "How am I to find the perfect man who deserves my love, or the unfailing friend who deserves my confidence? Where can laws be found which will assure the peace and happiness of my country? Where and in what occupation am I to achieve happiness myself?" No one can reply to those who state their problems in this way.

What are the questions that should be asked? "Where am I to find a person with weaknesses like my own, but with whom, thanks to our good intentions, a shelter from the world and its changes may be erected? What are the hard-won virtues necessary to a nation's existence? To what work can I devote my time and strength, thus forgetting my fears and regrets with the help of discipline? Finally, what sort of happiness shall I be able to achieve, and by whose love?"

There is no permanent equilibrium in human affairs. Faith, wisdom, and art allow one to attain it for a time; then outside influences and the soul's passions destroy it, and one must climb the rock again in the same manner. This vacillation round a fixed point is life, and the certainty that such a point exists, is happiness. As the most ardent love, if one analyzes its separate moments, is made up of innumerable minute conflicts settled invariably by fidelity, so happiness, if one reduces it to its important elements, is made up of struggles and anguish, and always saved by hope.

Set in Olympus, an Alphatype
adaptation of Trump Medieval.
Printed on Hallmark Eggshell Book paper.
Designed by Beth Hedstrom.